Temples
and Fields

POEMS BY
PHILLIS LEVIN

Temples and Fields

Temples and Fields

POEMS BY

PHILLIS LEVIN

The University of Georgia Press

ATHENS AND LONDON

© 1988 by Phillis Levin
Published by the University of Georgia Press
Athens, Georgia 30602
All rights reserved
Designed by Betty McDaniel
Set in Palatino
The paper in this book meets the guidelines for
permanence and durability of the Committee on
Production Guidelines for Book Longevity of the
Council on Library Resources.

Printed in the United States of America

92 91 90 89 88   5 4 3 2 1

Library of Congress Cataloging in Publication Data

Levin, Phillis, 1954–
Temples and fields: poems / by Phillis Levin.
    p.   cm. — (Contemporary poetry series)
        ISBN 0-8203-1052-2 (alk. paper).
        ISBN 0-8203-1053-0 (pbk.: alk. paper)
    I. Title.   II. Series: Contemporary poetry series
        (University of Georgia Press)
            PS3562.E88966T46 1988
        811'.54—dc19   88-4822
                    CIP

British Library Cataloging in Publication Data available

For Toshiko
and in memory of my grandparents

The publication of this book is supported by a grant from the National Endowment for the Arts, a federal agency.

Acknowledgments

The author and publisher gratefully acknowledge the following publications in which these poems, sometimes in earlier versions, first appeared:

Agni: "The Stairwell"
Antioch Review: "Something About Windows"
Boulevard: "Chalk and Ash," "A Song," "Dark Horse," "Indian Restaurant," "A Meeting of Friends," "Inscriptions"
Denver Quarterly: "Clearing Over Clouds," "Everything Has Its History," "Springtime Soliloquy"
Grand Street: "The Skaters," "The Ransom"
Hubbub: "Cobblestone Path Through the Park," "Voices Through Rain"
The Nation: "The Cricket"
The New Criterion: "Rilke's Nightfall"
New England Review and Bread Loaf Quarterly: "What the Intern Saw," "The Brooklyn Botanic Garden"
The New York Arts Journal: "Winter Sculpture"
Paris Review: "The Lost Bee"
Partisan Review: "The Little Boy Who Fell," "Out of Chaos," "Prisoners' Round"
Pequod: "Citizens & Sky," "The Way to Mount Aetna," "Ore," "Another Defense"
Poetry: "Grace," "Machines," "On Marble"
Poetry Review: "Animals," "The Shadow Returns"
Shenandoah: "After a Summer of Ancient Greek"
Southwest Review: "Autumn Book," "The Border Guard"
Virginia Quarterly Review: "The Paperweight"

"Lunch After Ruins" first appeared in *Secret Destinations: Writers on Travel* (Pequod/Persea). "Helen Keller: The First Day" was printed for the inaugural program of The Helen Merrell Lynd Colloquium at

Sarah Lawrence College. "The Coin" originally appeared in *Skeins*, a chapbook published by Dogwood Press.

A portion of this book was featured in *PN Review* (Great Britain).

The following poems were reprinted in the *Anthology of Magazine Verse & Yearbook of American Poetry*: "Everything Has Its History" (1981 edition); "Something About Windows" (1985 edition); "Machines" and "Out of Chaos" (1986/87 edition). "Rilke's Nightfall" also appeared in the *Annual Survey of American Poetry: 1986 Edition*.

The epigraph is taken from *The Great Wall of China* by Franz Kafka, translated by Willa and Edwin Muir, copyright © 1946, 1974, and is used by permission of Schocken Books, Inc. Excerpt from "The Maimed Man" from *Collected Poems 1919–1976* by Allen Tate. Copyright © 1977 by Allen Tate. Reprinted by permission of Farrar, Straus and Giroux, Inc.

I wish to thank the Ingram Merrill Foundation, the MacDowell Colony, and the Virginia Center for the Creative Arts for their generous support. My special thanks go to Elfie Raymond, Christopher Ricks, Jean Valentine, Molly Peacock, and Dana Gioia for their encouragement and criticism. I also want to thank Gloria Glickstein for her advice.

Contents

Leopards break into the temple and drink the sacrificial chalices dry; this occurs repeatedly, again and again: finally it can be reckoned upon beforehand and becomes a part of the ceremony.

FRANZ KAFKA

One

Something About Windows

In the distance are the horses,
In the distance is the noon.
The moon is a long way off, a long time.
When did space separate
From the meticulous counting down
Of beginning leaf and scattered petal?

Pauses, sirens, dust, pollen, light.
It is spring, but none before like this.
What to make of conversations flickering,
Playing in and out of meaning
With an ease that bears resemblance
To the congenial balance of sun and shade.

She, who sits at the table next,
Extols the intricate layers a salad
Can hide to entice and surprise,
Subtle and cool as a banker's eyes.
He chooses from the menu without wonder;
No hurry, the day is far from over.

But what was that green change
Crossing his retina?
Just a woman's back, covered
In mint—her silk shirt's fluctuation
As she strides past kids on bicycles,
Graphic in their perfection.

Freed from longing
For my face in another, feeling
Diffuses through this sheet of glass,
Where forgetfulness and memory kiss
Without falling for each other.
Yet there is something about windows

That makes me want to tell
The story of my past:
How I traced the life of a raindrop
As it raced to the sill,
How a wish split the wishbone
And the truth divided.

The sky was once suspended
By silver chords of sound.
But I couldn't wait
Till it was over, till the flat
Four-cornered room of childhood
Ended, as the globe came into sight
And my hand extended.

The Skaters

One wears what the other weaves: a quickening
Dance of flame across the man-made pond,
Composing a pair unlikely to bear
Each other up in any circle
But this ring, where ordinary motions
Freeze and drop like winter rain fallen
Among the evergreens; what we expect
From one another briefly rises
To the surface through those smooth figures sketched
In ice in a code impossible
To break—except by weaving the same course,
And then unwinding, and winding back
Threads that cannot tie, yet trip and trick
Couples who move in time outside the rink.

On land, what they decipher would mean less
Than a spider's web glistening in frost.

Just as we part, the half-sun silhouettes
Two figures sailing close until they miss.

The Ransom

Without knowing
How or why, I was standing in a square,
Meeting with a high-placed officer

Who said I'd been selected as the go-between
To bring a ransom set upon the head
Of one I didn't know and never would.

I took the job and promised to deliver
The sack of cash; then slept in a fever,
And woke immersed in duty and the hour

The thing I had to do would be fulfilled.
People assembled at the chosen spot;
I approached them, ready to play my part,

When a voice in the gathering called out,
"They've changed the producer!" The producer?
The words, null and void, were loud and clear.

"But this is life," I said, clinging to sense:
"No one produces it. It's not a show."
They didn't understand my point of view.

In medias res (as if a god had died),
A world dissolved and roles were reassigned
For reasons that remain unspecified.

So there I stood while someone else went on:
No practiced understudy or rising star,
Just the result of a shift in power;

A change that came to pass not for anything
I'd done—no fatal flaw in character,
Sickness of soul, was the root of the matter—

Only a minor detour in the plot,
That a producer new to the scene
Had cut the part played by the go-between.

What could I do but swallow my pride
And walk away (I wasn't paranoid)
After handing back the bag of loot,

Another worthless prop, for all I knew.
Birds were singing, buds flaring in the blue,
So why should I mourn? But what of the life

Of one unknown—without a face or name—
Whose strangeness was becoming what I am.
Better to turn to the natural world,

Following a twist in nature's plot, than live
Where youth is a decoy and time a ruse
Sowing the grass with rue. Before I choose

To drink the bitter draught of history,
I'll hail the tragic muse; then drain the glass,
And put out all the lights and watch the news.

Grace

Someone across the room laughs so lightly
We hear the rustle of pines, the rattle
In a cone when a sparrow, alighting,
Leaves for a reason unsung in its singing,
And the air, stirred by startled breath, now
Emptied, surprises like another's pain
We register without a smile or gesture,
Admitting it is there as our pupils
Dilate slightly, change gently pulling like
An undertow anemones answer
When waters whose whispers are lost in waves
Intimate worlds we will never enter.

A.D.

On the long night train from Nice to Rome
My love and I sat side by side;
The sky distilled, the earth grew redder,
My love and I could love no better.

We spoke in silence, pausing for stars,
Breathing the dust of millions of hours;
Mountains of light through windows shone
—It was not a gold triumphal tone,

But the dark music of empires scattered,
Cries of dogs and horses startled
By sudden changes in the realm.
At the midnight stop in Genoa station

Dull black suits and battered valises
Illustrated the broken tale
Of deals gone sour for a poor trader
Whose wife limped down the narrow aisle,

Then posed behind him, a wooden icon.
As he hoisted up the trunk of possession
She sank in the only seat that was free,
Squeezing together my love and me.

He stood the whole time, waiting for Rome,
In the August heat his sweat ran down;
She sat through the ride with a sober stare,
The feet of her children waded the air.

At dawn we saw the mantle of Maria
Unfurling in the amber wash of Roma;
We were wound in the wheels of the holy city
By the time the train pulled into anno Domini.

To Rome

City of man, your terminal is a shrine
Where every eager tourist finds a sign,
Shadowy deflections from the cross
Infinitely glinting off the railway ties;

Your body is the blueprint of a time
When adumbrations of a passing cloud
Proved every child to be a child of God,
And every year the first year of our Lord.

Lunch After Ruins

The arcade of the ropemaker's cave
Dripped and echoed:
Ceiling of moss and quartz,
Reverberating pool of recurring rings.
Then a lemon touched my shadow
And cool steps carried my feet
Back to the streets of Siracusa.

I stopped her with *Ho fame,*
The guidebook's phrase for hunger.
She mumbled, *Sinistra,*
And I followed—not a direction
But the veil over her eyes,
The black dress, the soothing pace
Of syllables after stones.

On the arm
Of my momentary mother,
I entered the trattoria
And ate bright fish
Just parted from the sea.

The Way to Mount Aetna

On the way to Mount Aetna,
Painted in white,
JOHN F KENNEDY
Pierces the night—

Spelled in the scrawl
Of a giant child
Against the dense
Volcanic wall.

December is mild,
The road climbs slow,
The sky funnels
To Dante's hell,

The slope ascending
From fig to pine,
Seasons coiling
The helix of time.

Safe in the shell
Of a foreign car,
We speed through ash
To feast on fire:

Homage and wonder
For a cheap thrill,
Sicily's Christmas
An orange spill

From the first temple's
Echoing cone—
God on top
With a megaphone,

Spouting for reasons
Deeper than ire,
Searing the lemon
And melting our tires.

We wait for a spark;
The forecast fails.
But spiraling through
The ancient dark

A snowflake blooms
And falls and falls,
Breaking the spell
Of the oracles.

Chalk and Ash

Make me a mixture of chalk and ash, I said
    To the one who stole into my sleeping room.
If you can enter without a knock or cry,
    Then I have the right to demand
A token of your presence, some sign.

Why do you want what all will become one day?
    When death cleans the slate and levels the land,
Turning the world to chalk and ash,
    Never will darkness again meet light,
Never will light show the work of the hand.

Then make me a whistle of chalk and play
    Notes that carry my hope past all regret,
Build me a raft of ash
    And blow it across
Seas of endless blue and endless loss.

There is no song in chalk,
    No sail in ash.
But with your blood I'll mix the chalk into clay,
    And with your breath I'll make the ashes dance
Into the forms that take your breath away.

My mouth is ash, my body chalk, and I
    Have come this night to leave you what I am:
Thirst and hunger for things you want to know,
    Chalk and ashes for things you have to say.
You shall taste chalk and ash every day.

Two

Springtime Soliloquy

"This way madness lies,"
The reasonable bird cries.
But what if the reasonable
Bird is mad? Made in heaven
We are not. Unbearable
Origins bear us up.
Another suicide
Or accident of birth
Shakes the hourglass.
April's tree outlines
The bare necessity
Of rooting oneself
Before straining
Upward. Why else fall
To our knees, supplicant
In worms and dirt,
Hands (unfolding
Leaves) bearing gifts
From a land our lips
Cannot pronounce.
                    Anger
Is still our song,
But all the brilliant halls
Are gone. Immortal one,
Recall our savage birth
That we may find
The law of death less cruel
Than mornings spent
On loss. Drugs and sleep
Patrol the daily life,
Barring joy and grief.
Words the truth could tell

Harden into stone,
Building a castle
Of forgotten tongues.
No beast struggles
In the net more furiously
Than a creature intent
On killing the divine,
Or reaching it in arms
Too human for such love.

The Temple Leopard

You taste my body's power when you run:
It carries you forward, a brutal hymn.
In twists and turns desire spins
Infinite springs, concentric, in my thighs.

But who would trust the yellow of my eye
Or dare to sleep while I sleep, you wonder.
But whose arms take you from hunger
When you pause outside the bronze temple door?

Animals

They burst in upon us,
Not asking for space or
Time to pause before time
Paces round and claws them,
Not knowing what in us
Is frozen by their stare
Answering the air.

We need them to show us,
In all their array—plumes
White and blue, spots, horns, quills—
How sharp cries through trees still
Spark terror, rouse in us
Arched eyebrows, carved portals,
The elegant clause.

Machines

Disassembled, outmoded, unattended,
What used to be useful glimmers through dust,
Heaped in shop windows, multiplying shadows
After hours, so soundless that defeat
Haunts hollow ears with surges of what was,
For a time, the dirge of all unuttered.

Here lie the mechanisms past regret.
The autumn leaves will pile up to the door,
Drifts of snow will darken into cinder,
Wheels will spin and rivers freeze once more,
But if we fail to summon spring in winter
The cedars will stand for what we forget.

Machines have their own seasons, revolving
Around us, though nature is not their fulcrum.
They too move beyond repair to neglect,
But cannot die like a diving falcon
Or repeat, in the end, names that inflect
As the sum of one's parts stops working.

Unconverted by death, they know nothing
Of the glory of noise and the daily
Trade of the ugly and the beautiful
We have listened to, in stories of many
For whom engines were passions, and the feel
Of life the sense of a great sound building.

Cobblestone Path Through the Park

Gradations of gray, alight
In late spring, take on the depth
And heat of surprise.

Seeds flee their leaves,
Leaves hang low, trailing
Shadows that skim these stones.

The difference between
What is worth noting
And what is worth nothing

Disappears into the elms.
Around the square, startled birds
Flee from the shadows

That fall from our clothes,
And dive into pools
Where their notes die.

Bits of glass, like breadcrumbs
Until nightfall, lead us
To the crumbling

Brim of a fountain
Filled by outstretched arms
Green with age,

Where we long to drink
From a naked girl
Whose hands will always be open.

Everything Has Its History

In the common day I find a common fact:
The chair in which I sit,
The small wood table,
The sienna vase
Lie mute in my room
As if they belonged here
Before I moved in.
But I know
I moved them in.
This chair occupies the space
I once needed
To fill with a chair:
Chair-space I called it.
I hunted for it.
When I found it, I carried it home.
I sat and read and ate
In a new thing.
I was new, I was made new.
Now I sit here remembering
There was a moment of love
Between myself and the place I inhabit.

Helios

A sky the inmost blue of flame,
Dazzling grasses scything the plain,
And up there an eternal savagery

Spanning what distances, what centuries,
With no more comprehension or recompense
Than now, in the fierce dispassionate sight

Of an eagle eating the sun.
Is this an image of Prometheus
Suffering the harsh sentence of Zeus?

Or Zeus in metamorphosis—
Casting himself at the forge of myth,
The solitary star that kindles earth.

How strange it is to flower into light
For beings who flee from darkness into night,
Feeding on fleeting gods that shine and fall
Faster than tears the sun unseals from snow.

A Song

Deep in summer I saw an owl
With maggots swarming through its flesh;
In autumn through bright hills of leaves
I found a bird with body torn;
I fed the deer and let the bread
Fall to the ground into the dust
As winter hardened the earth's crust;
I found their antlers in the grass
Beside the smallest flower of spring.

In joy and terror I woke each day
To meet this strange familiar friend,
Silent, playful, shrieking, holy;
In joy and terror I woke each day
To study its face with eyes and hands,
And it was soon my private study;
With joy and terror we fill each day,
In joy and terror the mouth shall sing:
The earth in love and death is our ring.

Another Defense

A place to go
Unlike where you've been:
Not the usual chatter
Among chameleons
And peaks of Camelot.

How far we've strayed
From fingertips of shade
And bleak prophetic birds.
Haven't you heard?
Almost nothing is left.

Here's the sublime
Antidote for grief unfelt.
Days of droning news
Drain away our lives
And strip the blowing tree.

Whoever goes
On this journey embarks
With human eyes and ears:
Sick of sham,
In need of no apology.

Inscriptions

We begin with a name: that has meaning.
Then there are stones, a patch of moss,

A hill of ivy leading to a door.
Who answers, who calls out to you?

Next, a simple feast: blackberries
Dangle over your head as you swallow

Milk, the seed of a pear, gazing
Into summer's face as you watch

An ant make its way up a blade of grass
Whose curve holds the secret of a smile.

Corners, alleys, windows, and walls
Engender the cloud-breaking span

Of an esplanade that your legs
Survey with long, hopeful steps

Before the desire to sink or the fear
Of shadows taints the air's rhapsody.

And even in the city, ruddy light
Blushes between buildings, gilding

Wrought-iron gates, collapsing love seats,
The rigging of street signs, clotheslines,

Mangled, noble trash-heaps of disrepair.
Night's retinue of piercing cries

(Or was it laughter?) scours the sky,
Clearing the stage for dawn: a barefoot,

Star-struck beggar calling for change
In the grand style, while frenzied talk

Of money and mastery buttresses
A symphonic highway sustaining those

Who clumsily or gracefully make it
Across failure's fantastic lacunae.

All at once certain words recur
(Bird, angel, cup, monster, time),

And we are numb or ablaze as names
Ricochet, settle in, gleaming

In a dream's dim sanctuary,
Susurrating reliquary

Where enemies and beloved guests
Huddle together to see at last

What cannot be seen—for we hold
In the hand what makes the hand

Tremble, possess, relinquish the gift.

Three

What the Intern Saw

I

He saw a face swollen beyond ugliness
Of one who just a year ago
Was Adonis
Practicing routines of rapture:

A boy who could appear
To dodge the touch of time,
Immortal or immune—
A patient in a gown,
Almost gone.

II

In the beautiful school of medicine
He read about human suffering,
An unendurable drama
Until the screen of anaesthesia
And penicillin's manna.

But now, in myriad sheets
Of storefront glass refracting evening's
Razor blue, in a land of the freely
Estranged from the dead, he meets
That face and fear seizes his body.

III

His feet have carried him to bed.
He thinks he must be getting old
To so revise
His nature and his plan.

He shuts his eyes
And in his sleep he sees a gleaming bar,
The shore of pain.
It isn't far.
People live there.

Rilke's Nightfall

You asked so little: only that one day
A rose be named after you; and today,
After last night's musings, in this summer
That returns me to you—still swimming
In the wave that first pulled me to the long
Flowing script of your elegies, the whorled
Shell of your sonnets, the ebb and flow
Of knowledge and loss in the halting cadence
A body assumes as the shoreline is claimed
By the tide—today I have come up
With a name, though I haven't yet planted
The flower, and am far from finding a plot
For the garden that will nourish and sustain
The light of this new rose, Rilke's Nightfall.

Indian Restaurant

Her weariness does not show,
Except when she pushes a strand
Of hair from her cheek before lifting
The spatula to turn the singed chappati.

"The people must support the revolution,"
Intones ths static-charged radio;
Darjeeling mixes with cream
And makes a pleasing spiral in my cup.

Though civilizations choke each other,
Morning restores horizons
Resilient as law—lines irrefragable
For as long as the sun effuses its corona.

What is my right, who does not work enough
And sleeps disturbed by noises, not by God?
I will enjoy the taste of this warm bread,
Hinting at bitterness beneath the edge.

Some would not change a detail of the world;
Have I the strength to lift it into song?
—To praise this girl whose brow is marked
With the weight of an ash, a tear from the dark.

Citizens & Sky

The city branching blindly through the clouds,
Its stream of walls, its flame of flashing glass,
Its buildings without wonder, windowless.
Aghast, the heartbeat booming underground.

There's something in the air: a currency
Whose random courses sweep us into crowds.
Beyond the fog our trees are grazing in,
Glitter gulls on errands from the sea.

Just now a jet broke through, clearing over
This geometric wave, these figures, bent
On getting home, colliding in blossoms
Without design, dissolving into sound.

The Brooklyn Botanic Garden

There was a rabbit face at dusk
And a double row of benches

Collecting in a shadow
Through which our footsteps tunneled.

The full moon
Dropped through a cloud,

Making me remember how you blinked
When a drop of rain

Hit your cheek, and I kissed it
Before it could fall,

Later wondering if it would have fallen
Or just disappeared.

Then we were trying to kiss
With our eyes open,

The dark pools
Deepening into each other

Until we could see
The second of loss closing in.

Running through this first snow
Past the frozen pond,

What comes back is
How we spoke of spring returning

The water lilies
As we watched them slowly

Dying last autumn,
When I began to want you in my life

And confuse you
With the yellow lily.

The Coin

The stones are green.
Green stars
Swirl up from the riverbed
Where I lean and drink
Until my face is water
In cupped hands.

A cricket erases
The skip of my heart.
Without my name
Between your teeth
I am empty as a green glass sea.

I drop a coin—
My wish breaks into rings:
I want and *I want* and *I want*
And you only can hold me
Whole under the stars
Falling as one falling
From earth to earth.

Voices Through Rain

Voices through rain do not dismember sorrow
Or send it packing.
Voices through rain, in which echoes echo,
Do not die.
I have seen how clouds,
Drifting into mist,
Lose definition, then brighten.

Who, looking up
At a half gray, half blue sky,
Has not wanted
To enter the blue, burst from the bounds
Of the body attracted to gray?

Some time or another, depending on who you are,
You may provoke yourself into being another
And find, strangely,
How much of what changes changes
Depending on the day.

For we are in a boat together,
Crossing into a country
Where nothing is going to be the same,
Crossing into a country
Where what was familiar
Will suddenly filter
Through voices through rain.

The Shadow Returns

Saw my shadow on the wall,
Saw my shadow, saw it fall
And renew itself with light.

It was my death that stung my sight:
Substantial time to race my heart
Before I turned from it in doubt.

It was my love upon the bed
Who pointed out my silhouette,
Anonymous and monochrome.

Never understood, till then,
The subtle bond of ghost and kin,
The visible world invisibles win.

Into the evening far sounds came,
Like laughter of people after tea
Rising to brush the crumbs away—

They always sounded false and thin,
Almost evil, estranged from pain,
But now this sound was part of me
And I was part of the world again.

The Stairwell

The deepening glissando of steps
Where the bannister spokes became a harp
On which my untuned song was played,
At night became the shrine of my unfolding,
A meeting place for dreams on the sublime.
In the dark, I rose from my bed
And moved across the threshold of my door
Into the hall, where the stairwell
Shone in the glow of the night-light.
At the top of the staircase I posed
Like a diver, held my breath and jumped
The full flight, hitting the landing,
Then gliding and floating through the house,
Lifted by the flare and fission
Of a thousand thoughts.
                         The stairwell
Was my night garden, where I returned,
By day, to bask in the light
And shadow of the spokes, considering
Generations of cloud shapes
Recurring like rhythms I strummed on the harp
While I sat at the bottom of the stairs,
Chin on the railing's lustrous wood,
Fingers flying swiftly on resistant strings,
Making music hollow as an echo.
There I plucked the fruits of isolation
And reason, for there logic took its turns,
A philosophy was born, and the disobedience
To a life which seemed the pale shadow
Of my dreams.
                  But the world that moves
All worlds imagined was shifting and teeming

Outside, where a tall pine grew,
Knocking against the second-story window
By the time I was ten. By then
I was done with hunting for treasure
In dirt and dead needles under that tree
And instead, in the heat of summer,
Descended to the basement, where thick-bodied
Books with thin, fine pages cooled
The spaces between my fingers; and upstairs,
In autumn and winter and spring, reading
In the parlor by the light of the bronze
Torch lamp, alone in the embrace
Of grandfather's armchair, I'd turn
To face its old, broad back—tracing,
In the network of cracked leather,
A faded map whose veins
Led through wavering tributaries
To countries and cities
Where I was explorer and ruler, unaware
That my world was unpeopled
And bare.
            So children are brought
From the womb into various lights
And darks, barely distinguishing
The forms and terms of their imprisonment,
But imagining, wherever there is a space
Resembling the mind (or a simple thing
Well-wrought), a new world—that does not
Breed and bury what should be cleared
And uncovered. For the way of growth
Is wound in a spring
Of information and viscera
Invisibly weaving patterns
The loving and watchful beholder
Divines. Looking in the mirror,
The child sees the beautiful petal

Of its face, reaches with the hands,
And begins to search the planet
For something that will match
This consciousness: first in the mirror,
Then in the window, the winding walkway,
The opus of light and air.
                              So to live
In a world shutting out
The danger at every turn of being
Alive is to rent a room doomed
To destruction by collapse or explosion.
The mind finds the analogue
For implosion in itself, for expansion
In itself; and soon the imagination
Sketches and fills in
A design that seems the blueprint
Of a memory—and thus, unwittingly,
Engineers the ruin of the prison
Before it has even been named.
The roof creaks open and folds back
Like an antique book, leaving the house
Utterly exposed to earth and sky.
Now the skull must cover
What the brain recovers, the heart
Regulate the rhythm of its rage
Inside its scaffolding of labor and desire—
Less a function of traffic and dread,
More the correlative of body and head.
Root systems: cosmology of coils and knots
That, in time, unravel and untwine,
Raying upward, where stars tangle
In the moonlit twigs, limbs bow
Under changing leaves, death visits
And departs, sunlight always casting shadows
In the mind's corridors, its beckoning
Branches and abysmal mines.

                              The self unwinds
To let the world be wound in all its ways;
The body reclaims the valley of the soul,
And from its rich well of darkness
Seeks the blue uncharted regions of day.

Four

A Meeting of Friends

Although their hair is turning gray
  They're tall and blue:
A white silk scarf, a strain of Bach
  Is what is new.

The beautiful now calmly shines
  Where once it fled,
The terror of their innocence
  Is almost dead.

They meet for lunch this time of year
  And always find
The brightness that their boyhood held
  Not far behind;

And though the distance that they keep
  Estranges others,
They share a dark, unsettled plain
  Like brothers.

When does a life begin to form
  And carry out
A silent vow the tongue cannot
  Articulate:

A line that travels, wavers, breaks,
  And then returns
As if the changes surfacing
  Were in the plans.

Why speak of men who look so glad
   And know their worth,
Settling inside their lives
   This side of death—

Have I been sent to sit all day
   And figure out
The true relations flickering
   Between two hearts?

Or do the truest feelings
   Lie on this leaf,
Where stories fit together,
   Unfolding grief.

One always holds a few words back,
   The other smiles;
Smoke curls through music as they talk
   Of work and miles;

For still they save what is not said
   Until the end,
When things untold turn into things
   Never meant.

On the border of the future
   Broods the infinite:
There knowledge slowly sips her wine
   And savors it.

But time is a stranger entering
   Without a sound,
And love is a stream changing course
   Underground.

It Is Found

In a crack in the sidewalk,
Flecks of light on a forest floor,
Or a violet vein running
Through a child's marble cheek;

In the law that links
The muted underside of leaves
To their glossy counterpart;
In the private life glimpsed

In a lake bottom's revelation,
Or sparks that carry strangers
Into realms of relation;
In phrases caught in passing,

Thrown back and forth each day
Until they solidify
Like landmarks that meant little
Before the dark of travel;

In names and faces forming
With the clarity and speed
Of the first drops of a storm;
And when the rain falls

It becomes a basin
In which the rain falls,
And seasoned as the skin of a drum
It calls and calls.

Helen Keller: The First Day

And the earth was without form, and void;
and darkness was upon the face of the deep.

No song . . . no green . . .
And wind and darkness
All that ring.

Always a falling of leaves,
Even in spring—lightning
The only blue.

Stopped by a blade of grass:
Its slow curve
A chord . . . then a bud

Quick as braille—
That chill the first day
Water was sweet,
Your dare warm in my palm.

The Little Boy Who Fell

The little boy who fell into the well
Must mine the darkening measure
Scaling the moss-fed rocks to a future
Neither President nor Pope can foretell.

The helicopter carrying the head
Of state circles a world the sun obscures,
Though moonlight casts up coins and stars
The little boy, until his falling, counted,

Wondering, wide awake in bed,
How many and how far they are that fall,
Whistling like spinning tops until
They blur into their speed

Before they lean and teeter,
Nodding the way grandmama does as she falls
Fast asleep in her chair.
He was pulled from a dream by the bells

This morning, remembering a murmur,
Mother murmured, lives inside a chamber
Of his heart—how he hears his heartbeat beat
Like a cricket caught

And shuts his eyes tight to concentrate
His fear into a creature
Whose limbs he smashes when they sprout
Sharp shards of ice greener

Than the grass
Tickling his face—
O mother, it is so far,
O father, it is so deep,

And so unlike your bodies
It is cold and steep,
Not a place for sleep,
A mute and monstrous

Darkness in which hunger
Feeds on terror
When your voices
Warm no longer

One who,
Unreturned to day's bottomless
Blue, swims in a slow motion race
Through measures of unmeasure,

In himself a buried treasure.

Prisoners' Round

after the etching by Gustave Doré
and the painting by Vincent van Gogh

Every day they file into the courtyard,
And gathering round into the round
Each, in his turn, is caught
In the morning light—
Like numbers on a clock
With a turning face
And broken hands,
Or a teeming waterwheel
Groaning in the sun.

Anointed by this light, one
Forgets they are prisoners
Facing another day: the sun
Out of their picture,
The walls drawn close and blue,
While the yellow of a dandelion
Seeps through cement
Cracked with a hunger
We attribute to things that kill.

Winter Sculpture

Words disappear as smoke,
Over a white hill, floats,
Then settles into snow.
We trespass and do not remember.

Days fall like this, lost
Between the crystal and its melt.
Stars reel and we believe
We are still: we go,
Whirling through night like snow.

Clearing Over Clouds

Sheep pressing toward the sun
In search of a master—
What have we to give them?

Untenable space, gray and molten,
Hangs in a parched pavilion
Called memory. Our pastures unfold

For us on parchment illuminated
With swollen signs, fruits
A different landscape

Offers. And we release
What we can lose without losing
Too much light, for it hurts

To believe nothing and no one
Knows how to read our music;
It hurts to believe

These sheep so thick and bright
With hunger live for this light
And cloud us from it,

Their eyes hidden, black
And heavy with truth:
Is it food or god

They seek and see
Far in the fluency
Of their kingdom.

The Paperweight

At times I wake to find my form
Lodging a world gone white
And hot as she turns me over
In her large hands, shaking

Snow from my glass bottom sea.
She wants this storm inside me.
Outside, the air around her face
Blurs, she sifts into dots of dusk,

Holds my smooth rind tight. I cool,
Clear, then she looks far—searching
My settled heart: families of trees,
Stones, houses (things we hold

In common as bodies of water).
She houses people, too; but hers
Detach, fall, move out. I am full,
Have no desire for open space,

Am set in my solution, contained,
Content to weigh down a single
Bed of pages. For I comprise
The stillness she wants to break,

Getting out of her heavy head
The storm she loves to make.
Transfixed, for an instant
She sees herself in me:

Her *self,* imagine that alive
In me—a raveled growth,
Its pattern out of place
Like a monstrous flake

With no sense to float, dissolve,
Or stay put. She'd never fit.
I could not live with her
That way, her weight within.

The Cricket

As we were walking
Down a hill of summer light,
In a country where everything
Is beautiful, a cricket
Fell to earth. The click
Of its carapace cut our pace.
Your mother turned around
And so did you. "Phillis
Stepped on it?" The translation
Came through: as if this tall
American brought trouble
Wherever she went. But no,
It only fell from a tree
In a suburb of Tokyo;
Nothing was to blame,
No cause in sight, unless
We hold the breeze
Responsible.
                    Nothing
In any language, any cry,
Comes near the noise it made:
It was the sound of death,
Death's rattle, an ugly,
Bloodless, insect battle.
It whirred around,
Like a toy a child had wound
Too tight, destroying itself
With its own motion: a final
Alarm, a frantic animal
Mimicking the centuries
In cycle. On and on it went,
Time pierced, all syllables

Absurd, as we stood together
On summer's hill, hearing
Its crude refrain transcribed
In the signature of redundant,
Mechanical pain.

The Border Guard

In the twilight, in the hot sun,
In the forest of buried nightmares,
In the grand hotel, in the brief glance,
I have found there is a loose thread
That unravels under my careful eye.

Nothing escapes my skilled receptivity
To heat, light, sound;
Bursts of rhetoric, pathetic stories,
Comic replies stick to the strip
Of my query like flies
When I stand at attention, ready
To remind whoever forgets there is
A ratio of authority, a limit, a line.

Love is not what I am after,
So put away those looks;
Neither cash, nor sailing ships,
Nor fantastic currencies of wonder
Can change my posture.
The will, the set mouth, the steel door
Bear witness to transformations
Brilliant and hard to grasp as distant gods.

Yes, everywhere are signs of transcendence,
Bargains, eternities, death throes, beasts.

Five

Ore

At the center of life
Waits an emptiness:
Baskets we wove
For fruit and wood
Filled only with air.
Many have wept for this;
They had reason to moan.
Who would have thought,
After cloudcarts and carnivals,
It all would stop,
A stark, frozen
Funeral after harvest.
The sun goes down at noon,
Language wanes.
Great spaces between stars
Fail to startle.
The end of life
Occurs in the middle,
When we must walk
Through sandstorms, sleet,
And falling roofs, wrapped
In a cloak of silence,
Blessing joyless emblems,
The difficult journey ahead.

On Marble

Was liquid once that, smooth or coarse,
Though cool now to the cheek, embeds
In ignorance its igneous past,
Being made of what it was not: the cut slabs
Displaying shells locked in cold embrace,
Lightning on water, darkest onyx
Glinting in sluices of rose.

Through exposure to other
Types—Travertines pearl-green as lichen,
Spring dawns of Rosa do Monte, Parians
Opaline white—one learns to distinguish
Stones expressing such variety
That the range within one kind may seem more
Disparate than the difference between kinds.

Yet, despite extremes of shade,
Texture, density, its present state portrays
Its change of nature: the enunciation
Of time's heat and pressure congealing
Into beauty resulting simply
From streaks of impurities spread
When the earth was an accident pouring.

So this stunning Rorschach, garbled
Mass of fire and ice, unintended
Pathos of natural formations,
Bespeaks—the way certain sounds and faces,
Rather than dissolving or merging,
Remain intact, constant as imperfections,
Anachronistic as eyes.

Materials

after reading Mandelbaum's Aeneid

On a shore where no one walks
The wind makes waves of sand;
Cries of crossing birds,
The crashing of the tide
Before and afterwards
Are one aubade.

Freed from euphony
The egg returns to the sea,
Coral multiply,
Kelp arch and coil
As the arc of a breaker snaps
And flags to blue.

By night's calculus
A ship reads its course,
Stars flash and fall
Into the forms left home,
But in the silent sky
A black horse burns.

In the chill of his purpose
Aeneas sleeps,
The eyelid hardening
Into a shield,
The past a weapon
That lifts and sinks

Inside his head.
Sails unravel and thread
Their mast—a needle
Forging the line to Rome:
Penelope's thimble
History's crown.

After a Summer of Ancient Greek

Siracusa

The paradigms flare, their constant change
Informs the dragon of your brain
That you must kill or stay the same.

Far from the compass that you shook
(No more a pressed flower in someone's book)
You step through a garden, speechless and free:

Leaf and stone cast colossal shadows,
Gold and cerulean clash in the sun's slow
Fever—here where the ruins come alive

After a summer of ancient Greek.
A bus ride along the thrashing coast
Of this island of the Holy Ghost

Washes you, wakes you, erases *before*:
A lovely girl in front of you, her
School dress a wafer in the light,

Absentmindedly holds her pen
While the bus rattles and sways and starts.
In front of her is a gentleman

Whose white jacket receives a design
Recording his journey in sea-blue ink
Each time a jolt rocks her forward and back.

Zigzags and swirls fill the linen field—
She looks up a moment, sees what she's done:
Her dark eyes drop, the pen goes down,

The ball point clicks, she turns to discover
Whether anyone traces her to those lines,
And meets your eyes' conspiring laughter.

The veils of your eyelids exchange a vow,
The next stop comes, you enter the air
Linking your arms with *Buon giorno, Hello,*

As she crosses you to a shaded square,
Pointing out fountains and worn façades
Glossed by her dialect's endless cascade.

Like Narcissus bent over Nature's glass
(Before his kiss disturbs the surface)
You press against sound unrippled by sense,

Echoing consonants clearly lost
In undulations of a thousand vowels—
The world translated and newly blessed.

The two of you start up Babel's tower
With a dialogue bordering on pantomime:
She seems to be asking you where you're from,

You tell her you're an American,
And bits of elementary English
Break through Italian, bright as fish

Flashing in low arcs over a brook.
Trading names in each other's books
Under a date tree's upturned brush,

You glance at your notebooks' different lines,
Surprised they both carry the paradigms:
The shared gift of this alphabet

A fossil unearthing your common clay—
Though Sicily's pages are quadruled and pale
As snow-capped Aetna on a cloudless day,

And she prints an orchard of perfect rows
Without your margins, where blue meets red.
As if you dove into different seas

And rose past the waves with identical shells,
You fathom this instant the daylight deepens,
Grasping a fragment of Aristotle:

The things of friends are held in common.
But what is a friend—your other self?
Then how can your other self explain

The paradigm her face contains,
Stranger than a familiar refrain
Answering patterns in the rain—

Though practicing what you will soon forget
You part as easily as you met,
Walking together down Babel's tower

Before crossing the blue into desire.

The Lost Bee

As a lost bee returning to the hive . . .
ALLEN TATE

When I returned to the hive I was one
Among many, in a blistering hum.
A braid of air had brought me far from home
—Blinder than flowers, simpler than the sun,

Weaving through waves of incandescent curves
That offered what they always had to give.
Then why suddenly did the hive seem a grave,
The queen, in her mystery, an end to serve

Who before was my mother, my god?
What happened on the way, and how did I lose
Direction, season, aim—scanning the skies
Numbly for a current, a sequence, a strand.

They welcomed me back with a typical dance,
But its fantastic patterns made no sense;
And yet I know, now, a tempo that encodes
The temples and fields, the pulse of time and space.

I must have been exiled from habit
By a strange wind, a stray leaf, a migration
Constellating unheard-of combinations;
But they don't notice, they don't mention it.

Their honey is too sweet, the hive too dark,
The swarm of cells too tight; and who can I tell
Or fly with?—for nothing we make can seal
The knowledge vaulting outside the matriarch.

In the flurry and buzz of business meetings
All that we hear is a forecast of trouble:
The comb's overcrowded, the queen's gold bubble
Polluted by pollen clouding her wings.

She's laid plans for starting a new colony
To restore our nectar's profit and destroy
The sting of death, decay, and anarchy.
Our empire's estate of wax and honey

Will thrive again, one day; and it is rumored
That I have been destined to attend
The queen on her odyssey—she trusts me,
Or perhaps she has grown sick of loyalty.

Autumn Book

Over the dumb and flawless plain
The sparrow trails its shadow, rain
Pardons the absolute, lightning
Splices night to night.
And gone with green
Is the absence of green,
A hum of black bees
Rising from the yellow leaves.

Dark Horse

For Włodzimierz Ksiazek

Like a child's cut-out, she holds her weight
Against the stiff, encroaching cold,
Standing so none may pass without
Gleaning the gravity of her load.

The wooden fence warps slightly; flakes
Cleave where shadows fall; her black skin,
Dense as winter silence, invokes
The long interval before she'll turn.

Resounding signs of sudden thaw
In rising tones of dripping snow
Compose deep caverns enclosing dawn,
Uncoiling secrets vast and slow.

Come walk inside this blinding space
And know it is made of ears and eyes
Compounding years of clouds and ice,
Dry leaves sighing through wind and tears.

Then if the centuries seem too sad,
The world withholding its love and shame,
Study this dark horse in a field
Who bows her head to time.

Night Coach

From the window of a train
The moon appears and flees,
A brilliant silent film
Cut up by winter trees.

A child approaching two
Wakes mother from her nap
And crawls onto my lap
To get a better view.

Breaking into speech
She taps the windowpane:
This is the first full moon
That she will try to reach.

Seated across the aisle
Man and woman smile
At infant in papoose;
A Mediterranean face

Bends over it and coos,
"Bambino, little one"—
The beautiful, foreign
Father a child would choose.

Kindness everywhere grows
In limited quantities,
But the borders close,
The fountains freeze,

And the brightest halo
Shrinks to a shadow
Gray as a noose.
Intangible truths

Vie with cruelty
For untranslatable bread.
Oh God, let us be free,
We call out to no god—

What else can be said
To sparse stars overhead,
Lighting up the home
Of a darker dark?

The train runs on its track.
Together and alone
The tossing sleepers moan;
Nothing answers back.

Out of Chaos

No wonder some prefer a narrow hall,
A single room where doubts die
Until possibility, that odd flower,
Returns its face.

The doors close and open every day.

The doors close and open every day
And every day we hurtle toward the city.

Today I saw the usual human disaster:
Head in her chest, legs pocked with pink wounds,
Fingers wrapped tight around a white handbag.

Then the subway doors opened and children
Piled in: the whole car filled with their high
Broken music.

At the next stop they all poured out;
The car was vacant, solemn, the air
Settled and clear—but she was still there.

Outside a lilac bush blows to the wind,

And everywhere one looks
A pre-Socratic flux
Streams down avenues
Of taxicabs and radios,
Mortality's parade crowned with neon and chrome—

As if we were beasts evolving toward a sentence
That breaks and disperses before we arrive
At the city we promised to build.

The Contemporary Poetry Series

EDITED BY PAUL ZIMMER

The Contemporary Poetry Series

EDITED BY BIN RAMKE